1988

❖ Cardinal Points

Winner of the Iowa Poetry Prize

Cardinal Points

Poems by

Michael Pettit

University of Iowa Press

Iowa City

University of Iowa Press, Iowa City 52242

Printed in the United States of America

First edition, 1988

Design by Richard Hendel
Typesetting by G & S Typesetters, Austin, Texas
Printing and binding by Versa Press, East Peoria, Illinois

The author would like to thank the National Endowment for the Arts for a fellowship which made the completion of this book possible. Grateful acknowledgment is also made to the following publications in which some of these poems first appeared: *Agni Review, Chicago Review, Denver Quarterly, Ironwood, Kenyon Review, Massachusetts Review, Missouri Review, Morrow Anthology of Younger American Poets, New Virginia Review, Ohio Review, Poetry Northwest, Southern Humanities Review, Southern Review, Three Rivers Poetry Journal.*

Library of Congress Cataloging-in-Publication Data

Pettit, Michael.
   Cardinal points: poems / Michael Pettit. — 1st ed.
      p.   cm.
   ISBN 0-87745-205-9.   ISBN 0-87745-206-7 (pbk.)
   I. Title.
PS3566.E89C37   1988
811'.54—dc19   88-14797
                                              CIP

for Dara

Who but the loved know love's a faring-forth?
                                        —Roethke

❖ Contents

*Publication of this book
was made possible by a
generous grant from the
University of Iowa Foundation*

Things take place instantaneously, but there's a long process to be gone through first. What you get when something happens is only the explosion, and the second before that the spark. But everything happens according to law—and with the full consent and collaboration of the whole cosmos.

—Henry Miller

panta rhei

—Heraclitus

❖ Cardinal Points

❖ Woman Jumping from Rock to Rock
Plate 170, *Animal Locomotion*, Eadweard Muybridge

The one-winged bird walks: flight requires balance
or else momentum. Think of the convict
crashing downhill through saplings and briars
toward the river where he'll lose the dogs,
howling at the hot scent each stumble leaves.
Does he throw himself away from his past—
striped shirt ripped off—or forward to freedom?
And this lovely half-dressed woman jumping
from rock to rock, as across a small brook?
Behind on the bank her lover calls out
Take care, take care. But the wine and water
are all she hears. Tumbling song. As she sails
from one rock, from one delicate ankle,
to the next, her arms rise in a flourish
that helps to steady her and dismiss him.
O how his clean unflappable jaw dropped
when she stripped down to her slip and was gone.
This quick rocky stream suits her spirit:
she sings out in flight her song of danger.
Just ahead the feathered green willows swing
in the wind. She will slip into that deep
shadowed world and let the wine take her off
into sleep. Where, in dreams, he'll come crashing
to her, breathless, stripped by and to desire.

❖ Sunday Stroll

Who is this man out walking
his miniature horse on a leash?
It trots by his knee to keep up,
too small for the smallest child.
And who's the woman with him,
pushing a pram down the strict sidewalk?
All along Main Avenue the azaleas
are opening their vivid eyes
to watch, amazed. In the stroller
sits a little black dog too happy
to behave. He chirps like a bird
and birds chirp back. Purple martins
in the air, robins on the lawns.
And why not happy? The sun and wind
are warm; Easter with its resurrection
and parade is only two weeks away.
At any moment the double oak doors
of the First Baptist Church of Northport
will swing open to the bright
mysterious world where my friend,
his wife, his tiny horse, and dog
stroll along serene and sanctified.
Where is it they go? I remember
one morning in Mexico, turning
a corner, coming upon a man and woman
wrestling a squealing hog
down the steep cobblestone street.
He had a stout rope to pull;
she had the hog's curly, crappy tail.
They'd heave together, get nowhere

and have to stop. Breathing hard,
they wiped their sweaty faces
and sat on the hog. All three rested
together. *Vamos al matadero*
the man told me. *We are going
to the butcher* he said, smiling,
scratching the hog's pink ear
as the sun poured its benediction down.

Driving rain falls from a sky
clear one moment ago. Where was I?
Across 13th Street the trees
are gray and blue with rain
blown by winds spun from the dark center
of a storm I never saw approaching.
Thunder is cracking, red and yellow
leaves scattering down the street.
I was drifting, lost
in *Evening on a Canadian Lake*, 1905,
where Remington has two trappers
paddle the edge of dark
and light, half his canvas the black
of a deep Canadian forest,
half the sharp beautiful blue
of a still lake. With their reflections,
with their birchbark canoe lit,
with their faces aglow like candle flames
at dusk, the trappers pass across the lake
in perfect silence. They seem to look
past my left shoulder. What do they see?
They won't say and I can tell
they go days without speaking,
their only language their movements
and those, too, silent as possible.
Between them—on provisions for their lives
apart from everyone—rides a dog.

Where was I? It was Washington,
white city of monuments
and buildings, each one waving Old Glory,
each one aiming and awaiting
its missile. It was December and cold.
Inside the gallery the heavy crowd
pressed ahead to see what in their lifetimes
they might never again see: A New World,
Masterpieces of American Painting.
Everyone—diplomats, bureaucrats, tourists—
was pressing, their lives threatened.
The white marble buildings,
the ones outside and the one we were in,
kept no one safe. The crowd pushed
forward, against the shoulders and backs
of strangers, as if that brought comfort.
It did not, though it brought us closer.
So it was a cluster of troubled human faces
the trappers would have seen beyond me
as I stood there, looking over
a stranger's shoulder. Small wonder
men seek the wilderness, where
the dark shoreline holds no danger
and the sky in the water is clear,
lifting the trappers up, emblems
of peace, golden in the center
of evening on a Canadian lake.
Small wonder we drift and are lost.

❖ Pavlov's Dog

Last night, late, a light rain
beading the windshield,
I held you and we listened
to the static and old songs on the radio.
Filled with the past, the failure
of love to last, beyond our breath
on the glass I saw coming
down the wet street a great dog,
his chestnut coat long and curling,
soaked as though he'd walked all night
to stand there before us.
I held you close and watched him
shut his yellow eyes
and shake slowly his massive head,
water slinging from his muzzle
in threads of light.
I watched him drive the muscles
of his neck and shoulders,
his back, flanks, hips a blur
of motion and water flowering.

And so I believed
love and sorrow must be foreign
to each other, the heart so large
they never meet, never speak.
Why is it not so? Why the old song,
desire and heartbreak we can sing
word for word after all these years?
Why as I held you did that dog
appear and seem to shake clean,

only to roll his eyes open
and stand unmoving, staring our way
through the rain? Cold and steady
and long into the night it fell,
into his thick coat, into my heart
where you walk, filled with love
and unafraid. I am afraid. Of Pavlov,
of his bell and saliva at work
in my life. Tell me how I am
to join you, to shake free for good
of that cold man's rain,
his dog standing wet, obedient,
and brutal as a bell ringing,
always ringing, for sorrow.

❖ So Long, Tuscaloosa

I give you the eleven lights
of Lurleen B. Wallace Boulevard north
to the Northport Bridge.
I give them to you strung
above the intersections, rocking
in the night wind, red smiles of hookers
making the same promise block
by block. I give you their light
filling the windows of stores gone broke,
skidding across oil slicks in parking lots,
streaking the creamy white Cadillacs
of Druid City Ambulance Service.
I give them to you through the rain
or under the influence: red-eyed, thick-tongued.
I give you expressionist smears
or the acute realism of a December night
so cold those lights would crack
if ever they changed color.
There's a law: the first light turns red
as you arrive. You can count on
twelve empty seconds watching
as they switch in sequence and you idle,
exhaust drifting through the intersection
and up the street. There's the fiery breath
of a dancing dragon twisting beneath
bright paper lights, but where, where
are the crowds of merry Chinese?
All you see are huge shadows
some college boy and his girl cast
on the windowless brick wall

of Bomar's Feed & Seed. I give you
their fierce quarrel, their arms shaking
shadows at the red, white, and black
Purina sign. I give you the silence
in your car, heater fan with its leaf
ticking like a meter. Home, you say.
That last resort. There is your chair
of self-examination, your bed
of doubt and dreams. I give you dreams.
Dream that you catch the eleven lights
of Lurleen B. Wallace Boulevard
just right, all of them green as trees
along the river. Dream you speed
under them, windshield turning yellow
too late to stop you. *Eleven, ten, nine*
you sing out, your eye fixed on
that last light, green, slinging you up
onto the Northport Bridge and out
over the black twisty river.

❖ The Flight Path

We move in. Next door they move out.
We watch their belongings go,
their loose ends. Through emptying rooms
screaming children race around
testing their mama's temper, her voice
after them like a switch.
Load by load, daddy fills the truck.
They'll be gone soon, gone back
to the dream town the little town
they left has become. What has them
going home could be anything, bad or good:
a job, death, 80 acres and a weathered house
that looks like heaven now.
Heaven here is filled with planes.
They take off and land incessantly,
thundering into the blue beyond the treetops
or whistling down toward white runways
too near to bear. It must be
what drives the little family away—
days in the shadow of their wings,
nights beneath their flashing lights.
How many, we wonder, did they last?
Atop a house of scrap wood and wire
the wound-up kids hammered together
and now, in love with their work,
hammer apart, their spotted dog barks
at every flight. From way up there
the faces at the 60 round windows
see nothing. Trees and roof tops receding
fast is all. No hello, no goodbye,

no wondering where we go, or why.
It's up to us down here to wish
those leaving good luck with the past,
that dream they return to. They drive off,
little left behind but a scattering
of pecans, green, shook loose by the planes
going over and over. It's up to us
here to stay put, and to last, to last.

❖ Man Performing Back Somersault
Plate 362, *Animal Locomotion*

Here's all the world's good news rolled into one
back flip. *Bingo* he sings: sudden money,
fame, friends, the beautiful girl who said yes.
A man like other men, he's delighted
with the promise fulfilled, unqualified
success. His spirits soar. Thus his muscles
tighten, spring him head over heels backwards
in a half tuck. When he lands on his feet
he thanks God for his run of luck. But what
of the leap against gravity and doubt,
Kierkegaard's somersault? What of the knight
of faith? Luckless, loveless, abandoned, he
stands naked before cameras that can't
record what in the heart sends him soaring.
They catch his arms swinging his body up
into the absurd. They frame him floating
in the air, a ball of muscle and bone,
but record no signs and wonders, no facts
before this fact of flight. Hard and finite,
the earth pulls him back down. Willing to break
his neck, the knight of faith will break nothing.
His despair, infinite resignation,
and faith remain intact. He'll land on earth,
ready for more bad news, the next back flip.

❖ Men Wrestling
Plate 902, *Animal Locomotion*

Two trim young Greeks evenly matched, wrestling
across the marble gymnasium floor,
their dispassionate master looking on—
if Muybridge had in mind's eye a drama
of pure motion, Attic grace, he was off
by miles. These two guys face one another
like heavyweights in some turn-of-the-century
Colorado mining town. They both sport
bushy mustaches, pot guts, meaty fists.
It's a bare knuckles brawl in Cripple Creek,
where the miners are out on strike and drunk,
waving their last poor wages and reeling
with despair. They see hero and villain,
Big Bill Haywood and the bad mine bosses
going at it toe to toe in the street.
Justice on their side, they bet the whole works—
money, the swaybacked horse they plan to ride
farther west, to Telluride where the mines
and whores are working. They plan to travel
on their winnings, on Big Bill's big left hand.
It shoots forward, misses, and their man's off
his feet, swung over a hip stunned face first
into the dust. The miners are dumbstruck
it's over so quick. Lucky they're so drunk
Big Bill going over backwards won't fix
in their minds or hearts. They're not beat, they say,
tipping the bottle back, no way, not yet.

❖ No Birds

This sunny early March morning
the wind rips in and the world swings, bare
golden willows, bones of lilacs,
withered mountain laurel. No birds,
the icy air is alone out there.
Not one red bud along the branches of the maple
thinks of opening. Not in this wind
that would tear your every breath away,
scatter it nowhere. No birds
want that. Let the bright ragged day
blow by, see what shakes loose:
leaves, a garbage can lid, papers, a hat.

❖ Sparrow of Española

Here's to that bedraggled sparrow
at the Sonic Drive-In
in Española, New Mexico, famous
Low Rider Capital of the World.
Sunday there is a holy day of cars;
the summer afternoon we passed through
all the discount auto parts stores
were open, their lots full,
and out on the drag a parade
of huge Dodges and souped-up Chevys
crept along, engines throbbing,
drivers in mirrored shades just visible
above the steering wheels made from chain,
the carpeted dashboards, soft dice
bouncing as car after car reared up
and dropped down, reared and dropped
like perfect black stallions
in movies at El Pasatiempo down the road.
Sunlight ricocheted off tinted windshields,
metallic-flake paint and chrome trim
as the drivers idled bumper to bumper
up and down U.S. 285, route
of the Pueblos, route of Escalante and Cortez,
of Spanish priests, American trappers, traders,
and tourists on their way somewhere else,
stopping for coffee, a bite to eat,
a tank of gas to get them out.
In Española the low riders drove all afternoon,
all evening, all their lives
for all we knew. For half an hour

we ate in our car and watched them go by
and go by. They were home there,
with the hard-luck sparrow
that accosted us at the Sonic:
small, brown, skinny, half its feathers
gone, others poking out
at odd angles, it looked ravaged
and incapable of flight,
sparrow of present misery forever.
Yet it flew, popping from beam to beam
holding up the corrugated steel roof
above us, flying about
or bouncing around on the ground, peeping
its one note over and over.
There, out of the hot sun
that bore down, crowning the cars out on the strip,
softening the asphalt everywhere
except in the shadow of the Sonic,
was home, was the known world:
cheap speakers squawking,
waitresses hustling trays, overheated
aroma of fries and tacos, crumbs
all the sparrows fought over.
Ours and the others of the flock—
those bigger, less tattered, maybe
not so hopelessly stuck in Española—
went begging shamelessly from car to car,
ours and the hot machines of low riders
in for a rest, a break in their ceaseless
16   revolutions up and down 285.

Give them tenacity. Here's to that
lost sparrow, that least bird
cheeping on the hood of our car, ornament
of desire that creates and defeats
failure. Here's to the insistent
call of its belly and heart
that won our hearts and tongues:
when we rolled out of the Sonic
into the parade and away
from Española forever, we were singing
its song over and over and over.

❖ The Uncompahgre Range

We wake to see
how everything reaches up

blue spruce and aspen
on the mountain, the mountain itself

ragged fields of snow above timberline
day by day cut

into new shapes by the summer sun
into stars, birds

a hand, one crooked white finger
pointing upward

We wake to see
the high eight-sided window

its clear and stained glass
filling with light

awakening stunned flies and bees
from their cold night

of sleep on its sill
so now they crawl about and sing

The fresh air beyond
is filled with a light snow blowing

we see when we rise
and stand, our faces to the window

from great cottonwoods
in full bloom along the river

its falling waters filling
with their flowers

and above all the white and black
wings of magpies

riding whirlwinds of cottonwood snow
noisy birds of joy

❖ Many Buddhists

Many Buddhists are marching along
our road. More Buddhists
than on other days. Most days
there is only one, a solitary pilgrim
in robes banging his drum
down the hill in the morning,
back up in early evening.
In town our Buddha-to-be
sits with begging bowl beneath a tree
and prays with anyone who will.
Many do. Many join him and chant
the lovely summer day away,
craving nothing. They follow
the Lesser Vehicle, Great Vehicle,
Diamond Vehicle and their long suffering
they leave behind. That's the idea.
Some unlucky days we miss entirely
their passing and the rhythm of our day
stretches toward them, tense
until they appear to relax us.
Today there are many, many.
More than we ever hoped for.
A traveling show along the shoulder of the road,
with prayer flags and a drum,
some in robes, others looking odd
looking so normal, every one a Buddhist!
As they tramp toward town, on her lawn
a little child is clapping, happy, happy—

from a startling white pagoda
on a hill not far from here
the Noble Eightfold Path runs
right past her house, right before her eyes.

❖ Mighty Sebastian Bach

At the ornate Sheridan Opera House
in tiny Telluride, Colorado
it's standing room only.
Some hoity chamber music ensemble from L.A.
has fled here into the cool mountains
with their flutes and violins,
their oboes, cellos, and whatnot
to play a plaintive sonata or two,
a ticklish concerto for harpsichord.
There's danger in listening
to Bach played live before your eyes—
the music would transport you
but the musicians cannot.
The harpsichordist hovering over his keys
in a wicked way. Violinists screwing up
their faces as if in anguish.
Balding cellist bored as he saws away.
All of them, you see, are
inescapably human, inescapably fleshy,
like you and the fellows to the left
and right of you. What anchors
our bodies are.
                    So you bless the A Minor
solo for flute and the flutist,
a woman so clearly taken by the lilting
line of Bach she follows completely,
her slim arms ascending, peaking
as her whole body sways under the silver flute
her lips kiss as she is lifted,
inescapably, into the dark rafters

of the Opera House, seeking
release, a way into the cool blue skies
above the mountains above the town—
no longer here, not yet there,
but lost above evergreens and lovely
snowy peaks—not yet ready, maybe never
ready, to descend, slowly,
by measures and single notes,
to this earth again.

❖ Los Alamos Rush Hour

How sunny I was, dreaming
of rainbow trout as I drove west
at dawn. Ahead, across the valley,
beyond the Rio Grande running full and muddy,
red banks green with cottonwoods and willows,
beyond White Rock and Los Alamos,
beyond the Valle Grande caldera,
high in the Jemez Mountains among evergreens
and pale budding aspen, frozen snow banks
softened, glowing in the early light
like embers. Dreaming, I could see
the first coal of ice break loose, sliding
a few feet down the mountain, a creek beginning
its daily rising, falling the miles
downstream to me. Fast as I could
I was on my way to the beyond—
San Antonio Creek or winding Rio de las Vacas
or wherever the fish sang to me
like angels in their silver robes.
Soon I would stand in the dazzling
water with them, my fluvial soul full,
singing back.
　　　　　　First, though, there was that
unexpected traffic, cars before me and behind
and more appearing from nowhere,
from Tesuque and Pojoque and who knew why
they filled the highway so early.
It was when I passed them and saw
pure science in the eyes of the drivers
I knew. Beyond their cold straightforward gaze

I could see formulas scratched on blackboards
in secure Tech Areas, breakthroughs
no one thought through, solutions
which would not come and nagged
their reasonable sleep. And I could see
their houses, children, lives left behind
early each morning for their work,
abstract and deadly. When I slowed,
they slowed, honked, passed me, faces
white, furious I would not go on.
Stupid drivers. Stupid commute
through the beauty of the desert,
stupid bridge across the river
and road up the arroyo to Los Alamos.
Caught fast in its traffic, unwilling
but increasing its number by one,
I could not dream into the distance
where angels in the Jemez sang.
I could not rush past those rushing there,
little city on its five mesas, icy hand
above us all. It would not thaw,
would not let go its awful grip.

❖ Sparrow Rousant

What is it—
when the black-throated sparrows are feeding
just outside my window,
dipping to the seed as the redwood feeder spins
slowly on its chain,
gold beads of millet in their black beaks
as they eye the quiet earth turning,
alert to danger and delight,
torn between seed and air—
what is it that has me
rise, throw my arms open,
grain spilling as the feeder rocks
wildly and the sparrows scatter, wings
rushing them who knows where?

❖ The Beyond

It is there your whole life
at your lips   your fingertips
waiting in the first light and breath
you take   blue   slick
wrapped in ribbons of blood   arrived
from a world within this one
into this one   this world beyond you

always   It was there before you
when   like some Cheyenne
pressing his ear to the earth to hear
what far off in the distance
what across the wide prairie was coming
your father into your mother's belly
leaned   his eyes in awe closed
better to hear her heart
and that tiny other heart beating
beating his way   The beyond

back there lies ahead of you
three long blocks up your street
a green bank rising
to the Santa Fe tracks   where after
the line of rattling freight cars passed
around a curve   out of sight
your flattened dime shined

ragged face of a tramp waving
taking the place of the cold perfect
face of Miss Liberty   now beyond

reclamation   It is past
over yonder above   the full moon
moving into view   sending its light forward
and following   into the dark circle
your telescope describes on the endless heavens
warm white edge of the moon
the thigh of the first girl you lay by
both of you untouched   waiting
for the other to begin   beyond worry

for the moment   all that mattered
before you   What faces you now you see
in the face of the old woman next door
leaning on her cane   descending
the five steps to her back lawn
to tend her perennial beds
or pin her lingerie to the line
You follow her motions   windows of her
house after dark flaming on   then off
as she makes her way to the bed
she may never rise from   her life
whole beyond the parts you know
She's close to the beyond

the great beyond some say
is no more than back   black ashes
of the body   returning to the fire
Believe otherwise   It is more
exceeding in degree any limit
you approach   It's the spirit
in the corner of your eye   racing from you
calling you forward as you turn
and turn and turn your whole life long
chasing what's beyond reach

like that blue wooden bird
set outside on the white fence   a wind toy
turning this way and that
in the breeze   all bright wings
spinning and dying as the wind gusts
and dies   getting nowhere fast   stuck
all summer under the fluid song
mockingbirds sing down from the roof peaks
before flying off over
the horizon   bound elsewhere   bound
beyond all hope or comprehension

❖ Elderly Man Lifting Log
Plate 382, *Animal Locomotion*

Guess what this aging gentleman looks for.
He squats, grips a round log, lifts one end high
above his head. With ease: either he's fit
or that thick log is light, riddled throughout
with decay. He peers beneath at the ground—
for what? He's some half-crazed, starving hermit
lost in the mountains for months, and he's watched
the grizzlies ripping rotting logs apart
for a feast of grubs, beetles, crickets, ants.
Perhaps in the flaked gold decay he'll find
a nest of young rabbits he'll skull and eat,
his first good meal in days. He needs the strength
to go on, to go on climbing over
the mountains, rock and evergreens, looking
for peace or apocalypse. He has seen
wonders: water falling a thousand feet,
centuries of rock, layers of time time
hasn't worn away. Yet. He sits gnawing
his rabbit, guessing which millennium
gave him the stone, dappled now with dried blood,
fur, bits of bone. Who or what will take him,
and when? Will he wake to find a grizzly
standing over him, lifting five black claws
into the starlight? Will he consider
a moment his life, his years on earth, then
rise to the five stars falling toward him,
delivering apocalypse and peace
at once, a blow like timber crashing down?

❖ Woman Turning and Lifting Train
Plate 232, *Animal Locomotion*

Let's put to rest any momentary
confusion: no big locomotive here.
Here is that haunting model who appears
in Woman Kneeling at Chair then Rising,
Woman Pirouetting, Woman Jumping
from Rock to Rock, and others. I've no doubt
she shined brightest in the eye Muybridge cast
over the men and women there to move
before him. He recognized her lovely
lasting form. Now my heart is set on her,
a woman long since risen to heaven
wearing only this transparent gown draped
around her hips. What she lifts here is sheer
as time, sheer as the imagination
that moves back, behind the twelve cameras
to stand with Muybridge. He's looking forward
to seeing these negatives: what beauty
they will show, they will show always. To me.
But put to rest the notion she's not real,
like that train nowhere in sight. She is real
now and was then, but in different ways,
in different eyes. Why I am so taken
with her is clear: nothing does not flow
from itself. Sheer skin cannot hold us in.

❖ Driving Lesson

Beside him in the old Ford pickup
that smelled of rope and grease and cattle feed,
sat my sister and I, ten and eight, big
now our grandfather would teach us
that powerful secret, how to drive.
Horizon of high mountain peaks visible
above the blue hood, steering wheel huge
in our hands, pedals at our toe-tips,
we heard his sure voice urge us
Give it gas, give it gas. Over the roar
of the engine our hearts banged
like never before and banged on
furiously in the silence after
we bucked and stalled the truck.
How infinitely empty it then seemed—
windy flat rangeland of silver-green
gramma grass dotted with blooming cactus
and jagged outcrops of red rock, beginnings
of the Sangre de Cristos fifty miles off.
All Guadalupe County, New Mexico,
nothing to hit, and we could not
get the damn thing going. Nothing to hit
was no help. It was not the mechanics
of accelerator and clutch, muscle and bone,
but our sheer unruly spirits
that kept us small with the great desire
to move the world by us, earth and sky
and all the earth and sky contained.
And how hard it was when,

after our grandfather who was a god

said *Let it out slow, slow* time and again
until we did and were at long last rolling
over the earth, his happy little angels,
how hard it was to listen
not to our own thrilled inner voices
saying *Go, go,* but to his saying
the *Good, good* we loved but also
the *Keep it in the ruts* we hated to hear.
How hard to hold to it—
single red vein of a ranch road
running out straight across the mesa,
blood we were bound to follow—
when what we wanted with all our hearts
was to scatter everywhere, everywhere.

❖ Virginia Evening

Just past dusk I passed Christiansburg,
cluster of lights sharpening
as the violet backdrop of the Blue Ridge
darkened. Not stars
but blue-black mountains rose
before me, rose like sleep
after hours of driving, hundreds of miles
blurred behind me. My eyelids
were so heavy but I could see
far ahead a summer thunderstorm flashing,
lightning sparking from cloud
to mountaintop. I drove toward it,
into the pass at Ironto, the dark
now deeper in the long steep grades,
heavy in the shadow of mountains weighted
with evergreens, with spruce, pine,
and cedar. How I wished to sleep
in that sweet air, which filled—
suddenly over a rise—with the small
lights of countless fireflies. Everywhere
they drifted, sweeping from the trees
down to the highway my headlights lit.
Fireflies blinked in the distance
and before my eyes, just before
the windshield struck them and they died.
Cold phosphorescent green, on the glass
their bodies clung like buds bursting
the clean line of a branch in spring.
How long it lasted, how many struck
and bloomed as I drove on, hypnotic

stare fixed on the road ahead, I can't say.
Beyond them, beyond their swarming
bright deaths came the rain, a shower
which fell like some dark blessing.
Imagine when I flicked the windshield wipers on
what an eerie glowing beauty faced me.
In that smeared, streaked light
diminished sweep by sweep you could have seen
my face. It was weary, shocked, awakened,
alive with wonder far after the blades and rain
swept clean the light of those lives
passed, like stars rolling over
the earth, now into other lives.

❖ Home Again

Do the hospital sheets cool
my father's face—swept with fever, unshaven,
a mystery immediately before me?
He speaks, incoherently, of years ago
as I ready the bowl of water,
soap, brush, and razor.
I shave that same face daily
thoughtlessly before the mirror,
but now I feel the mortal heat
of his cheek, touch again his rough beard
untouched since I was a child
swung up in his arms each weekday evening.
On alert after 5:30, I watched
from the limbs of the live oak out front
or listened in my room for the door
to swing open singing *Home again*
home again, jiggity jig. I lay in wait,
master of the distance between us, seeing him
standing in the aisle, bus rocking
away from the tall white buildings
and soaring bridge downtown.
Hand looped in the leather strap,
he sways from stop to stop up Canal Street
as weary shoppers and sales ladies rise
to exit at Claiborne, Broad, Carrollton.
Every movement is clear. At Metairie Road
he steps down in his suit and hat,
into the sunlight and heat, to wait
for his next ride. Beads of sweat gather
beneath his eyes and he loosens his tie,

leans back against a low fence,
the ten thousand bleached white tombs
of Metairie Cemetery shimmering behind him.
That last bus he takes daily
will come soon enough. Soon enough
it will take him past the blocks of dead
in their bright vaults and his stop
will come, bus doors folding back to give him
the white sidewalks of his own street.
Will I ever know what moves my father?
What desire beyond this—to walk,
tired and content, toward the distant
green oak where his son hides.
Toward his house, his front door,
the cool rooms where he will sing out
and lift me to his ruddy, rough face,
to the all-but-lost scent of after-shave
I breathe and will always remember.

❖ Louisiana New Year

Cold beneath our layers of camouflage,
far out in the marsh beyond Des Allemands,
long before dawn we waited, watching

the distant fires of refineries sputter.
On the dark waters around us decoys
swung into the wind, glass eyes cold

and unblinking. Wind rattled through
our blind of golden rosoe, bringing us
the staccato other-worldly night-cries

of muskrat and nutria, bringing sounds
from so far they had no source
except we dreamed one up. It was bleak

then, before night lifted, before
the half-light when ducks began calling
one to the other, male and female mallards,

whistling heavy-bodied pintails,
blue-winged teal that would begin flying
first, fast and low over the water.

Anticipation saved us, that long waiting
for a flight to appear anywhere
on the gray-gold horizon and to steer

toward us, to sight their own kind
rocking on the water calling up,
to bank and circle and at last open

their wings to us, whispering *Now!*
It saved us to lose ourselves looking,
eyes watering, the shivering we felt

no longer the cold marsh wind blowing
but our blood running fast within us,
its source far beyond our understanding.

When the day went flat, when in one summer morning
I'd done all there was to do
on the face of the earth—twelve blocks
I knew too well—when I'd traveled
to my borders and between, everything
exhausted as I sat on a curb, wondering
what in the world could fill the hours,

it was to the glowing yellow stacks
of *National Geographic* in the attic
that I turned. In the almost cool room
one bare low-watt bulb shined
toward the dark musty corners
as I slid one slim spine from the others.
Inside lay the mystery of the distant:

the moons of Jupiter, monkey temples
in Siam, the lives of Eskimos,
desert nomads and their nasty camels.
I left the old neighborhood behind,
traveling place to place—Kathmandu,
Madagascar, Machu Picchu—entranced,
anticipating what I knew lay ahead

on those waxy pages: the body
of some young African woman, her breasts
sagging with dust or gleaming
with oil, paint, intricate tattoos
I imagined I myself might fashion

with the touch of my palm
and the loud, loud drum of my heart.

At the edge of another world
whose fevers I did not know
but sensed I would suffer with pleasure,
in the half-dark attic my eyes opened
wide like the eyes of her children—
holding tiny bows or blowguns,
toeing the skull of a wild pig—

and I was revived, ready to hunt
the leafy backyards once more.
Silly games behind me, until dark
I dragged my warm belly over the earth
and breathed beyond its rich summer funk
the scent she left and I followed,
savage, new worlds now mine to conquer.

❖ Woman Emptying Bucket of Water on Seated Companion
Plate 408, *Animal Locomotion*

It's been tits and ass from the beginning,
lovely young women drenching one another
or flopping naked into bed. So sniffs
the critic, who has never in his life
known when to laugh. One stark naked woman
huddles in a tub. Her head bowed, she prays
the water won't be cold, prays her papa
in Minnesota will please never see
this photo. Up steps woman number two,
twice as naked. Her prop, a big bucket,
is filled with ice-cold water. When it hits
the girl in the tub darts up, nipples cold,
becoming the small dark eyes the critic
cannot turn away. *O Aphrodite*
rising from the sea. Or some abstraction
like that for this freezing Minnesota
girl. Let him see *her*, like bawdy Muybridge
behind his cameras, laughter booming,
Lovely, ladies, right lovely—undying
Art! Let the critic yearn and go to her,
flopped naked in the sun. Let him ask her
name, offer his coat. Let her thank him, *no.*

❖ Man Walking Downstairs Backwards, Turning,
   Walking Away While Carrying Rock
   Plate 151, *Animal Locomotion*

Life is so complicated, demanding
our full attention. This busy man eyes
his rock like a cook with a fresh soufflé
or a scientist with somebody's brains
to examine. All the while he's feeling
for that last step with his foot. Under stress,
his quirkiness becomes clear. On his head
is a black silk coolie cap, the same kind
worn by the Woman Walking Up Incline
Carrying One Bucket. They together
are our strange Jack and Jill. Imagine them
meeting, each naked as a stare but for
those little round caps and her sunglasses.
Did she think she'd go unnoticed, or what?
Jack had his eye on her from the first day.
Kindred spirit! Now, after work they meet
in a cafe, shy, slightly embarrassed
to see the other with clothes on. Why not,
they say, leaning over their tea, leave this
routine of act and photograph behind?
This knotty modern world's too perilous.
They'll simplify, take to the countryside.
They'll bring their oaken bucket and rock rock,
wear their black coolie caps and nothing else.
They'll stay one day or fashion a long life
free and easy . . . O wouldn't it be nice!

❖ Willows

Most romantic of trees,
we bow before their deep insatiable love
for water   voracious roots burrowing
into wells and sewer lines,
great black branching trunks
lifting prophetic limbs high
toward the cloud-streaked night sky,
and everywhere falling water—
long breeze-blown skeins of willow leaves
that are not tears, is not weeping
though we look to these willows
to comfort or cry with us
as we turn away from or face
the deep and eternal losses
our lives deliver us.

❖ Astral Life

Did I cry out in joy
as I climbed, a child two years old
exploring the high kitchen breakfront?
Did I shout from heaven?
So removed am I now, so distant,
all that was immediate then
is lost. I don't feel the hard wood
with my hands, elbows, and knees,
don't see the tops of things—
stove with its blue fires,
counters with their jars and knives,
my mother's startled look, her arms
reaching for me. And I've lost
what I was after, what drew me upward
to the new world of each shelf,
its dust and moths and rows of white china
plates that faced me and held my face.

Did I climb for the moon, the moon
which has no body and calls
for ours? Did I climb toward the night
years later I lay exhausted
on a cot in an echoing warehouse loft,
unable to unknot and sleep? I stared ahead
as behind me in a hundred warehouse windows
the bright moon rose. A hundred moons
rose and looked down on me,

their light filling the loft.
Then I left my body. I floated free.
In that gray cinderblock room lay my body
without me, the eyes open, covers
rising and falling with breath, a form
I no longer filled. In awe I backed away.
And saw there, outside the warehouse windows
looking in, another figure. My self again.
Again I backed away, and again,
from figure after figure, unnumbered
selves aligning below me as I moved
outward into the night, afraid,
uncertain I'd return through each one
to myself, that still form in the warehouse.
I would become some black moon
forever—lightless, unseen, watching.

What brought me back?
And when I did return, moving forward,
dropping through the skies, gathering
self after self, was I wrong to stop
in my trembling, cold body?
Falling from so far, I might have sought
the life deep in my breathing and heartbeat.
But I did not. I rose and hurried out,
away from that room, its windows
and its hundred setting moons,
never to know how far I might have gone
outside or within myself.

I might have reached the last star

or the first cell, but I could not
bear the loss, the lost body
left behind for someone to find,
to touch, but never again revive.

❖ Valentine Show at the Lingerie Shop

You adore this day dead-center
of the worst month of winter
given over to the heart. To roses,
chocolates, to these tokens
of affection. An outrageous redhead
and a blonde parade expensive intimates
before the husbands nudging one another,
crotches itching as they shift
in their seats and whisper. Classy,
this show. Sex dressed up nice,
not undressing. You still remember
the very sleazy barker outside
Topless Bottomless on Bourbon Street.
He pulled the door open and breathed
at you, passing by slowly getting
your eyeful: some stripper bumping her snatch
at the faces staring up from around
a tiny table trashed with weak drinks,
cigarettes, dollar tips. *No cover,*
no minimum he rasped in your hot ear
and you knew he meant your life
was empty without the nasty times
ahead inside. The pasties and g-string
gone. Topless, bottomless, the wild night
down to nothing. Down to the last black hour
when the heart breaks. But you know all that
is past, won't be back, so don't
drift off. It's February and maybe this

next bit of red and black lace and silk
on the chilly body of the blonde
is it, the gift you came here
on this cold night looking for.

❖ Petting Zoo

At night the empty shopping mall
fills with calls of the animals—

squawks and whistles birds let fly
from their cages, whinnies and bleats

from the mammals. The keeper snores
on the floor outside a dimestore.

By day the merchants do at best
a poor business. When people come

it's for discounts and attractions
like zoos or troupes of acrobats

or craftsmen in glass. Picture
a medieval market with a parking lot.

Here you'll find goats of every color
and their kids of still more colors,

a llama so soft hardened men bend
to rub a cheek against its flank,

and tiny ponies, a sleepy Jersey calf,
a peacock strutting back and forth

above a bobcat pacing its cage.
Black tongue pressing syllables out

against its hard yellow beak, a parrot
croaks the expected—*hello, hel-lo*—

and you are inside, admitted
by a man whose job is to sit, fat,

at the gate and sell tickets
or take inquiries about the job.

Two men—their faces young, restless,
vaguely dangerous—work the pens,

brooms and dustbins in hand,
heads bowed to the bright sawdust

where the neat scat of rabbits
lies like a prize. They flick it

away from the steps of children
wandering from beast to beast,

their hands extended, released
by mothers or fathers to go touch.

Wonder makes them move slowly
and some children cry, frightened,

clawing up the bodies of their parents.
As if from trees they see down below

a terrifying world of the unfamiliar
and the familiar made strange

by proximity. An African hornbill
on the fence opens its ebony wings

and wild beak wide. Or a baby goat
plants its hard little hooves

and licks, its tongue hysterical
over the sweet salty face of a child.

Echoing down the long light halls,
her happy screaming brings a crowd,

spectators who soon no longer
can resist. One by one they enter,

leaving their caution behind,
touching flesh to feather to hide,

to become one with the birds and beasts,
one with the human beings. Inside

everybody mills about, petting everything
in sight, their lives at last ecstatic

as they sing out and the zoo fills
to and beyond overflowing.

❖ March Thaw

All the venerable gray sugar maples
are tricked out in their finest rhinestones,
walking around in the rain, so pleased
with everything. Overnight each tree
has been hung with two or three or four
battered gleaming sap buckets,
the woods giving up its sweet secret
essence for almost nothing.
The mean radio says sleet by evening,
the temperature plummeting to zero.
Do those old women care? And me,
sitting under our leaky sunporch roof
I've got six tin cups and two coffee pots
catching cold rainwater drop by drop,
note by note. It's the song
of a child too young for words
so her spirit sings. It's wild runners
of honeysuckle blooming now
before the bitter weather comes back.

❖ House Move

Breath by breath
40 pneumatic jacks are raising
their stubby arms in the dark cellar
up toward the light. It comes
as a seam around them, a blazing geometry
they see and can't see past
as the house lifts. Wind spins
ancient dust over the cellar floor
and flowers bend their bright faces
down into the cool dark, *ooohing*.
They can see the little roots
they've woven through the earth
all these years. They've always wondered
where they stood, but never in their wildest
did they dream this—goodbyes
from their own house, perched on a truck
rolling up the road, up the hill,
waving and waving its doors and shutters.
Never, never did they dream this
enormous emptiness theirs now forever.

❖ Legless Boy Climbing in and out of Chair
Plate 538, *Animal Locomotion*

It seems a trick of lighting, his legs lost
only in shadow, not in fact. A stunt,
like a solar eclipse or Jesus missing
from the tomb. Astonishing, but you know
they'll be back. In fact, they won't. Imagine
the nights he can't sleep, the sheet that lies flat
just beyond his fingertips: fields of snow
stretching trackless before him, the fair girls
he will never have. On the street he spies
their hips swinging and remembers running
toward the freight car—the leap that falls short
by inches. He catches hold with his hands,
swings gracefully under the great iron wheels
that barely leave the track. He's left staring
across the rail at his legs. His blood flows
before him. His brother begins to scream
like a steam whistle. Now his mother says
The good Lord moves in mysterious ways.
Mr. Muybridge wants to take your picture.
See what a lucky, lucky boy you are!
On his face you see nothing but bitter
determination. There's no trick to this.

❖ Man Shadowboxing
Plate 344, *Animal Locomotion*

This tough, well-built boxer follows five plates
of lesser Men Boxing, all staged, hokey
as TV wrestling, not one solid blow struck.
The loser in Men Boxing and Knockout
slipped a punch and took a dive. Not so here.
This guy fights his tough, elusive shadow
on the up-and-up. They're beyond cheap bribes:
temptations of the flesh fail, all punches
land. See their heavy muscles flex, rolling
like massive shadows cumulous clouds cast
upon the earth below? We stand beneath
thunder and lightning powerless to stop
its heart-stopping boom and dazzle. It's death
we fear, divine judgment in the future
for some past act down here. So we are trapped,
battling shadows our own flesh and souls cast.
This solid fellow hasn't a chance: doom
will answer every bell he answers,
will match him blow for blow until he drops.

❖ Bad Back

In the office of the orthopedist,
the lame enter, each one worse off,
pain on their faces clear
as a smile. The dumb old joke of despair
goes, You know you're alive
if it hurts. Well, you're alive
and dying for it to end, suddenly
as it came—the twist and slight pop
of doom. Consider the range of movement
the needle now lodged in your nerve
rules out: dime on the street
you can't bend to pocket,
dog you can't stoop to pat,
basketball, dancing, love's loop-the-loops.
Consider the spirit, trapped
deep in your back, stiff or numb
or convulsed by turns. You watch
the arthritic old, the athletic young
leaning on their canes and crutches
as they file by, bent or gliding
to avoid moving. You aren't them
you tell yourself, you aren't them,
returning week by week or shuffling off
to the next doctor, the new sure cure.
Now the lunar ceilings of hospital halls
roll by above you, a landscape broken
by precise fluorescent lights,
silver heads of sprinklers,
faces in green or blue caps and masks

passing with half a glance down

at you, flat on your back. Your spirits
are too low to rise no matter
how soothing the orderly is
with his patter, how smooth on the turns.
He may be wheeling you gingerly
to that long-awaited time
you are healed, you are whole again,
but until that time it's no use,
no go for your soul, for the body
you don't want to hurt so bad.
All you want now is out.

❖ *The Fox Hunt*
—Winslow Homer, 1893

We have all seen in the sky
the black crow flapping away

from some tiny bird, enraged, attacking
from above, below, relentless

in its grief. And we've said good,
good for you. Painting this striking

scene of death to come, is that
what Homer felt? Sinister black wings

open against the slate-gray heavens,
from the cold sea come the crows,

rising from the horizon to hover
over drifted snow a red fox

labors through. Sunk to his belly,
one dark paw reaches forward

as he looks back at their approach,
backs of his ears black as their wings—

almost as though he reaches for them,
ready to embrace them, their talons

and beaks that would pick his eyes,
spill his blood. The red berries

Homer has painted suspended
above the snow on spare thorny stems

are the touch that tells us what
we may expect. Nothing more?

Above them, beyond the shivering
white surf hitting the rocky shore,

we in time will note another detail,
a great white bird made small by distance—

whether scavenging gull or crane
of paradise, we'll never know—

flying our way. As it must,
it will arrive too late. Afterwards.

After the soul of the fox is torn
from the body. Death is certain

to happen soon. By these elements—
red and white and black so ominous,

composed, and beautiful together—we see
how in his heart Homer struggled.

What against the many can one do,
save show your colors as you go?

❖ Furnace without End

Those bad winter nights
I'd lie listening
to the floor furnace
start and stop, flames
deep in the heart of it flaring,
burning a cycle, ceasing,
leaving the white-hot metal
to cool, tick like the wheel
of chance no carnival
is without. For over an hour
over and over in the night
its rhythm slowed, wound down
to the almost out,
the nearly silent,
when all at once the furnace
would kick in again
with its rumbling fires
and I'd shiver
at the sure sound of it.

❖ Boat-tailed Grackles

Out of sight in the trees grackles sing
their discordant, comic song:
check check check, wee-oo wee oo,
then that long rusty creak they loosen
like a nail. I remember elaborate plans
as a child in another, greener place:
shoebox on the lawn, twig and string,
line of bread crumbs to lead some bird,
small and light and lovely, out of the blue
into my trap, into my hands.
What would have happened
had I fooled one of *these?* Out of sight,
their eerie clacking is touching, inept
bravuras from the powdered bosom
of your sweet, eccentric, operatic aunt.
So when grackles drop from the skies—
oily feathers iridescent in the sunlight,
each one wary, a cold ochre eye
trained on the air above—it's you
who's fooled. Over the ground they flock
in circles like insane, like shocked
survivors of a catastrophic shelling
they fear is sure to start again.
Such anger, such harsh alarms they raise.
Lucky as a child to live beyond their range,
I never ran from hiding, never reached
my hands into a trap for so fierce a bird
as this. Had I seen directly before me
the ugly beak open, had I felt the body swell
and shudder as the death-rattle broke

from a grackle's throat, had one in my hands
cried out to the trees, the trees crying back,
branches lit with terrible black rainbows—
no doubt I would have flung those wings
far, far from me, out of sight,
out of all but memory.

❖ Footsteps

Up on the roof, tramping around
with his hammer in his hand
and his lips full of nails,
is the old carpenter
at his fitful work again.
I watched him go, smiling,
pigeon-toed, from truck to ladder
and up, his step light
on the wooden rungs.
Now I hear him walking
from here to there and back
on his business, his repairs.
I hear his stillnesses,
I hear his hammering.

In time I'll hear it stop
and he'll descend:
at the top of the window a brown shoe,
a leg, another leg, his waist
with its big leather belt of tools,
chest where his heart hammers,
his tanned hands and face,
its expression remote—

as if up there in the clear
cool November air with nothing
between the sun and the bright head of his nail,
he'd been thinking, thinking
of the gods that walk above
the blue ceiling above. As if

he'd been lost in their footsteps,
those they took instead of taking flight,
those they took when burdened,
when wondering what in the world
to do with him, with me,
with us all down here
at their mercy.

❖ Star Route, Box 2

Bearing this divine address
is a black mailbox breaking loose
from its cedar post. Weeds
poke up from the rocky ground below.
I'd say no one lives here
but its red flag is up
to the mailman, its red flag flies
with word of some wondrous event
or no event at all, I'll never know.
I should stop, I should open
the black mailbox and read it all—
feed and light bills, the note
to a sister in Michigan, the long letter
to a grandson serving overseas—
read it slowly, there in my car,
as if, bone-tired, I were now home,
the blue mountain lifting me
and my few good neighbors on the Star Route
high into the drifting clouds,
lifting me on clear nights up beyond
all the distant little lights on earth.

❖ Full Cry

If all motion is toward loss,
sound a wave
that flattens into silence,
light a wave,
touch a wave,
then you are right
to spend these last days
almost motionless,

in your chair saying little
while nurses cross the room
to the next darkened room
where your wife lies, stroke
you will never understand
holding her still,
no one letting go

but your heart moving back
to some cool and empty night
in the mountains of New Mexico,
fire an hour's walk
behind you, rough country
along the river between you
and what warmth,
what hands of green smoke
the mesquite coals now wave,

listening
through your blown white breath
for the dogs to begin,
for that first broken bawl
from the throat
and beyond the throat,

hearing them ignite,
high chop of the bluetick
and baying of the black-and-tan
driving the prey they desire
across the mesa's broken slope,
deep green cedars and piñon
scattered over moonlit red rimrock,
dogs' full cry

carrying forward
and back to you, still
so you can hear
as they race along the trail,
voices disappearing off
down the deep canyon, no way
you can follow, no matter—

though you've lost them,
you carry like a torch
in your hand an ivory horn
yellow, smooth
as a rock washed by the river

running to you and away
into the cool and empty night,

horn you can raise to your lips
to call them back,
call until they all come back.

❖ Girl Walking Towards Woman, Carrying Flower
Plate 465, *Animal Locomotion*

Believe for the moment
in this gift of flowers
the small girl holds out
as she walks forward,
fair and round, through sunlight.
She carries pearly everlastings
for the seated woman
whose face grows radiant,
whose bare arm rises to receive them
like Adam's hand for the touch
of God. It is God the Son
who will redeem us.
This gift the woman reaches for
is her own life returned to her,
the young life to live through,
the son or daughter we fear
too soon will turn away
and won't return, whose life will flower
beyond us, beyond our care
or understanding. We age in doubt
and memory, we can hardly imagine
life going on without us.
The pearly everlastings
touch the woman's heart
though they break it. The kiss
she would give in return
the child will not have. Fair
and sunlit, innocent and so immortal,
she turns away: no gift
so rooted in death is welcome.

❖ Cardinal Points

At the round earth's imagined corners blow
Your trumpets, angels, and arise, arise . . .
—John Donne

This is that one morning each long summer
I wait for, waking early to find
the air in my dark room cool,
finding on this late August morning renewal
in a breeze from Canada, arrived here
to revive me, to lift my spirit
like a leaf fluttering from the heat-weary trees outside,
the pecans, poplars, and oaks hanging over
13th Street, Tuscaloosa, Alabama.
Awake, I rise with the voice
of my daughter, who can sense daybreak approaching
and is all through sleeping peacefully
in her crib: under the wild galaxy
of painted wooden stars and planets,
hand-made angels and birds revolving together
like a dream beyond her reach,
she looks up at me—beaming, ready.

And so I lift her
out, past the yellow lightning bolt,
past space ship and shooting star
up into the skies and against my heart,
rattling its crib of ribs. She settles there,

warm, and in one another's arms
we travel through the quiet house
down the long shadowy hall to the front porch
to the red hammock where we swing
in the chilly dove-gray light and watch
the world come to life. Down 13th Street
an old ragpicker drags his sack of valuables
from can to can, rifling garbage and waving
as the paperboy rides by, winging
the news onto the neighbors' lawns, papers
gathering light, glowing fat and white
until the neighbors in their robes and slippers
appear and disappear, enlightened.
Above them, rightside up then upside down,
a gray squirrel runs the telephone lines, leaping
to the thin branches of a live oak he rattles
with all his might, awakening songbirds, cardinals
and mockingbirds that whistle greetings
back and forth, back and forth
as I tell Emily, on this first cool morning
of her life, of the heavens and earth.

Pink, grinning, quizzical, she listens,
or seems to, to facts I remember or invent
about stars: number, size, intensity, color.
Millions beyond those few thousand
the clearest summer night shows,
red, yellow, white, or blue they burn,
their burning their being. They live
as distant lights, and I give Emily names
of constellations we can see—Cassiopeia,
Lyra, Pegasus—and names of constellations
we can't—Nirvana, Valhalla, Heaven.
At this or any hour no telescope will do:
she must have faith in God, Brahma, Buddha,
in Zeus, Odin, Allah. Faith Seraphim
have six wings and surround the throne of Glory
chanting *holy holy holy*, faith
that below the Seraphim are Cherubim,
Powers, Dominions, Thrones, Archangels,
Angels. I tell her there are angels
over the tame and wild beasts, over humanity,
angels of annihilation and ascension,
angels of clouds, dawn, flame,
rarified air, thunder, terror, rains and rivers.

There is Raphael, angel of joy and knowledge,
and Michael the angel of chaos.
There are angels of mysteries, patience, sanctification,
angels of the abstract and concrete,
one angel hovering over
every green thing on earth, saying *Grow*.

There is no reason not to
so she believes me, and babbles
her long vowels over and over and makes
a sound that sounds like *day*. It's astonishing
she has come to me. Under our angels
together in our hammock we rock the sun up
above the trees as I point out to Emily
east, first of the five cardinal points,
the round world's four directions and inward.
Look east and there you'll see
our star, that warms us, lights
us and everything else—trees, houses, streets,
beer can blinking in the gutter,
spider webs shimmering in the St. Augustine,
gleam of light on the wind-flicked leaves—
our star turning the world its colors.
See, I say, nothing's untouched.

In our slow spinning round, we extend
from tiny Mercury and moony Jupiter
to Pluto, icy in its distant orbit.
And beyond. Yet we are not stars.
Out there in the deep purple red hot comets
whistle along, no one to hear, nothing
but the stray meteor or satellite
sent rocketing up from down here,
from the billion uplifted faces of the Chinese
or the eighty-odd thousand faces
of Tuscaloosa, hers and mine included.
Though farther, out there is like down here,
distance a question of degree not fact.
Venus and Mars or two men or one man
divided between his mind and heart—
the only difference is distance
touch might cross say we say *we must.*

To the south now a few clouds rise,
weather of heaven, toward the sun.
One hundred miles beyond our porch
the rocking gray-green waves of the Gulf of Mexico
are beginning to warm, warm winds
rolling up and clouds bouncing along—
wispy altocumulus or stormy cumulonimbus
that rumble inland steamy summer afternoons.

If this morning we could ride the clear zephyrs
that wrap the earth I'd show Emily
atmosphere and hydrosphere, geology and geography,
a thousand fields of study, lands
and peoples beyond our poor power
to comprehend. What is it they say?
In her room is the bright inflatable globe
Emily plays with, with its four blue oceans,
seven continents, big and little nations
painted pink and yellow and green.
It's a small toy and can't show the startling
blue lake in the mouth of a dead volcano
rising like a god from the rain forests, can't show
cities, towns, farms, fields plowed and fallow,
can't show the ragged armies arrayed
against the endless machines of death,
the small points of fire and the explosive clouds
and their shadows. Our burden is we can
see forward and back. It wasn't different then,
or there. The world opens continually,
has and will, whether in wounds or beauty:
shacks of the poor, riotous azaleas
across 13th Street—we look on and pray
our angels do not abandon us, do not despair
of the wreckage we choose when afraid
no one's there, no one watches over us.

Yesterday morning for what seemed hours
Emily and I rocked and watched
a road race, a long irregular line of runners
passing by before us. From the west,
led by a blue police cruiser—blue light
revolving in the early green heat,
cheerful cop touching his siren each intersection,
people up and down the block collecting
at the curb, Emily and me too—came four men
in wheelchairs. Spokes of their chrome wheels
spinning light like suns, they sped past
furiously, sweat on their faces and arms,
their legs useless or missing before them.
Cheers went up as their soaked backs
disappeared into the distance. I watched,
Emily in my arms, without words, what words
possible to explain or replace what was lost,
what remained. They were just gone
when the first runner—with long effortless strides,
barely touching the street himself—raced by,
five willowy others like him in their grace
not far behind. Soon we were seeing
scores, hundreds of runners, bodies and strides
so different it was hard to believe
they made the same motion. In turn
the first woman appeared, the first child.

Loose, bounding, shuffling, stomping the pavement
on their way, joggers came and went:
red hair, hat, tattoo, skinny and fat.
The first old soul appeared, the first
pale, panting face of agony,
and at last, the first runner walking,
a man no longer driving himself, penitent,
toward the finish line, the paper cups
and exhausted bodies scattered over the ground.
To Emily and me he grinned, said hello
in going by, made a face at his fate
and was gone, human, down 13th.

Toothless, drooling, delighted, shifting
to look as the cool wind shifts
and the wind-sock spins above us—a fish,
down its rainbow flanks little mirrors like scales
flashing—Emily hardly remembers
yesterday's heat. Here's the boreal wind
come to bring us another direction,
bring us the Arctic icecap, the snowfields
of Saskatchewan, where today a man is burning
a fire, bent to the flames, his breath
making yellow leaves dance from the kindling,
hiss of the white birch burning sounding
like a running stream. We step and do not step

into the same wind as he. North is the cold
we welcome coming: it's fat ducks
to the ricefields, hummingbirds to Mexico,
human beings into their houses, their beds,
their bodies in love breaking out
in sweat, their breath fog on the windows,
freezing overnight, white stars everywhere
when they wake. In this stiff breeze
Emily's eyes blink and shine like ice
under which lies the molten core of the earth.
What's a child, what glowing corridors
of embers and flame, fluent, elusive
as wind? She'll keep her secret forever
and I'll keep looking. Into this eager air
all the weathervanes aim their arrows,
like the points of every compass,
pulled north toward the cold that bears down
upon us, bearing the gift we lean into,
our bodies quickening.

Now we'll leave the red hammock rocking
without us and return, leave the street
to its movements and return, leave the wind
kissing the trembling surfaces of the earth
and return. Inward's the direction
we take last, without maps, wandering.

There are times at night when Emily cries out
and I tighten, and lie there coiled
while our lives orbit and I decide
what's wrong, or, after it grows quiet again,
Yes there are angels. Other times
what's there, in there—idea, dream, emotion—
carries us away, wheeling the body round
with or against our wishes. It's then
we make those corners. To stop ourselves.
To save ourselves. Here's the house,
here's the room, dim and cool as first thing
this morning. And here, rolled into one
corner is the world Emily now knows
according to her father. Almost round,
it is filled with my breath alone,
and a tiny leak lets out a steady, undetectable flow
into the house, and beyond, into the wind
that's here and gone. World always
in need of inspiration, world we can't let go
flat and immobile for fear we are wrong,
world where the angels come down to us,
I reach for it, I swear it is good,
and I give it, like a secret to keep forever
in a corner of her heart, to Emily.

The Iowa Poetry Prize Winners

1987

Elton Glaser, *Tropical Depressions*
Michael Pettit, *Cardinal Points*

Michael Pettit is assistant professor of English at Mount Holyoke College. Recipient of a National Endowment for the Arts fellowship in 1985, he is the author of one previous collection of poems, *American Light* (1984).